Italy

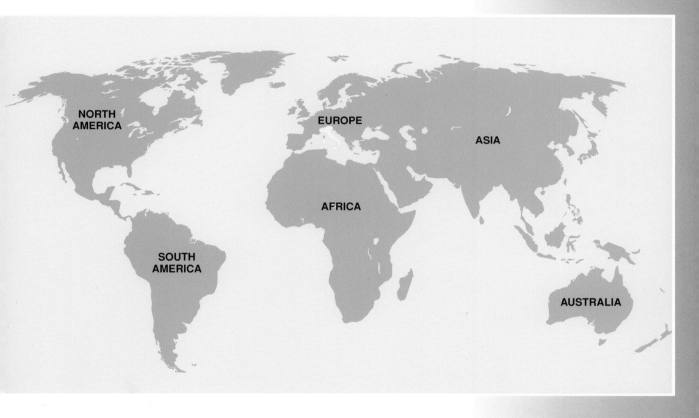

NORTH
AMERICA

EUROPE

ASIA

AFRICA

SOUTH
AMERICA

AUSTRALIA

Clare Boast

Heinemann
LIBRARY

First published in Great Britain by Heinemann Library
Halley Court, Jordan Hill, Oxford OX2 8EJ
a division of Reed Educational and Professional Publishing Ltd

OXFORD FLORENCE PRAGUE MADRID ATHENS
MELBOURNE AUCKLAND KUALA LUMPUR SINGAPORE TOKYO
IBADAN NAIROBI KAMPALA JOHANNESBURG GABORONE
PORTSMOUTH NH CHICAGO MEXICO CITY SAO PAULO

© Reed Educational and Professional Publishing Ltd 1998

Designed by AMR
Illustrations by Art Construction
Printed in Hong Kong by Wing King Tong Co. Ltd.

02 01
10 9 8 7 6 5 4 3

ISBN 0 431 04542 9

British Library Cataloguing in Publication Data

Boast, Clare
Step into Italy
1. Italy – Geography – Juvenile literature
I. Title II. Italy
914.5

Acknowledgements
The Publishers would like to thank the following for permission to reproduce photographs:
J Allan Cash Ltd pp.9, 10, 22; Trevor Clifford pp.12, 13, 15, 16, 17, 18, 21, 24, 27; Colorific!
B. & C. Alexander p.7, J. Blair p.11; Katz Pictures G. Berengo p.23, G. B. Gardin p.25, C. Paone
p.28; Trip B. Gadsby pp.7, 26, J. Moscrop p.8, C. Rennie pp.4, 19, H. Rogers p.4, H. Rooney p.29,
E. Smith pp.14, 20.

Cover photograph reproduced with permission of:
    background: Tony Stone Images, Michael Busselle
    child: Image Bank.

Our thanks to Betty Root for her comments in the preparation of this book.

Every effort has been made to contact copyright holders of any material reproduced in this
book. Any omissions will be rectified in subsequent printings if notice is given to the Publisher.

CONTENTS

INTRODUCTION

Italy sticks right out into the Mediterranean Sea and is shaped like a boot.

ITALY'S HISTORY

Nearly 2000 years ago Italy ruled most of Europe. The Italian city of Rome was the centre of the **Roman Empire**.

The Colosseum, in Rome, was used for shows during the Roman Empire.

In Siena, in the north of Italy, a horse race has been run each year for the past 600 years.

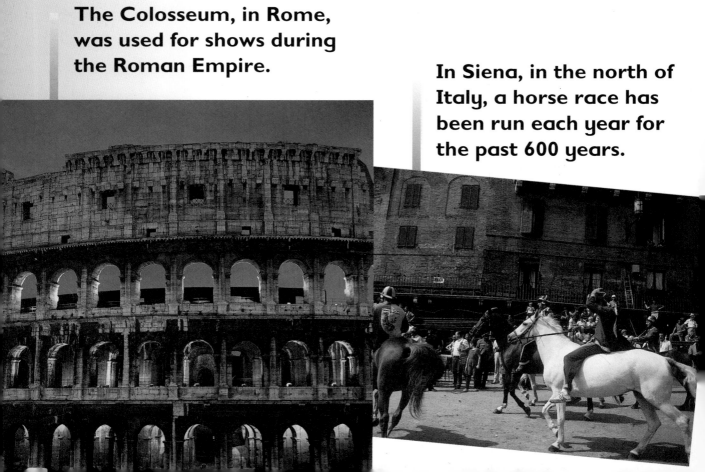

The Vatican City is where the Pope lives. He is head of the Roman Catholic Church.

After many wars, the Roman Empire broke up. Italy broke up, too, into lots of small countries. In 1861 most of these countries joined up again to make Italy. Even now there are two small, separate countries inside Italy. They are the Vatican City and San Marino.

Today the north of Italy is much richer than the south. Many people in the south make a living from farming.

THE LAND

Italy is a **peninsula** – it sticks right out into the Mediterranean Sea. The mountains in the north are called the Alps. The ones that run right down Italy like a spine are the Apennines.

RIVERS AND LOWLAND

The biggest rivers in Italy are in the north. They flow down from the Alps. The rivers in the south are smaller. Some of them dry up in the long hot summers.

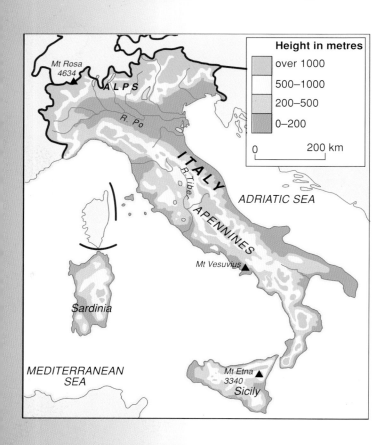

These mountains are in the Alps, which divide northern Italy from the rest of Europe.

No one lives in this village in the south of Italy now. Earthquakes made the buildings too dangerous to live in.

VOLCANOES AND EARTHQUAKES

Italy has one **active volcano**. It is called Mount Vesuvius. It last **erupted** in 1944. Italy also has earthquakes. During an earthquake the ground shakes. A big earthquake can shake down buildings and tear up roads.

WEATHER, PLANTS AND ANIMALS

THE WEATHER

Italy is a long country. Because the north and south of the country are far apart, the weather is very different.

The north is colder and wetter than the south, especially in the mountains. In the south it hardly rains at all in the summer.

Even northern Italy is hot in summer. The Lido, near Venice, is a popular northern holiday spot.

PLANTS AND ANIMALS

Much of the land in Italy is used for farming or industry. Only the very high or very dry places still have wild plants and trees. The mountains of the north have lots of chestnut, cypress and oak trees. The south is too hot and dry for trees like this. There are just bushes and short grass. But olive, orange and lemon trees are farmed in all but the wildest places.

There are not many wild animals left in Italy. Bears once lived in the mountains. They are nearly **extinct** now. There are still wolves, foxes and wild boar there.

Mount Etna is an extinct volcano on Sicily, an island in the south. Not much can grow there.

Watch out for poisonous vipers (snakes) and scorpions in Italy!

TOWNS AND CITIES

OLD TOWNS

Many of the towns and cities in Italy are very old. Some, like Rome, were built in the time of the **Roman Empire**. Others were built between 1400 and 1500, when Italy was also rich and powerful.

NEW BUILDINGS

As towns and cities grew, newer buildings and factories were built around the old centres. Many Italians work outside the old town centres. But the old towns are still very busy. They are full of **tourists** who have come to see the old buildings.

A square in Rome. Tourists visit Rome to see things built during the Roman Empire (like the Colosseum) and the Renaissance (like these buildings).

Lots of poor people live crammed into these old buildings. They live in tiny flats or just one room.

NAPLES

Most of the big towns and cities are in the north of Italy. But Naples is in the south.

It is the third largest city in Italy and has just over a million people. Rome, the capital, has almost 3 million people. Naples is one of the few industrial cities in the south. Lots of people have moved to Naples from the countryside. They have come looking for work. Most of them end up living in the poor, crowded parts of the city.

Towns and cities are important. But more than a quarter of Italians still live in the countryside.

LIVING IN FLORENCE

The family live in a flat near the town centre. Both parents work to pay for the flat and 2 cars.

The older boys catch the bus to school each morning.

THE DE ALFIERI FAMILY

Walter and Lucia De Alfieri live in the city of Florence. They have three boys, Vincenzo (who is fourteen years old), Guglielmo (who is eleven years old) and Federico (who is three years old).

THE FAMILY'S DAY

Walter and Lucia work full-time. Walter is a doctor. Lucia works for a book publisher. Vincenzo and Guglielmo go to school, while Federico goes to a nursery school. At the weekends the family can do things together.

Lucia buys some salami in a local shop.

The family like playing games or reading in the evenings. Even Federico joins in!

MEAL TIMES

Lucia does most of her shopping in the small shops near to their flat. She buys meat and vegetables there. She also buys bread, which Italians eat with every meal.

The family eat their main meal at about 8 o'clock in the evening. By then the sun has gone down and it is cooler. They often eat salad, pasta, meat and cheese.

The older boys like to row on the River Arno. The river runs through the centre of the old town.

FARMING IN ITALY

There are farms all over Italy. Farms in the north often grow different crops from farms in the south, because the land and the weather are so different. Some crops, like olives and tomatoes, are grown all over Italy.

Farmland near Florence. The farmer is growing grapes.

There are also vineyards all over Italy. They grow grapes that are made into wine.

FARMS IN THE NORTH

The biggest farms are in the north. Here there is enough rain and the soil is good. They grow wheat, potatoes, rice and other vegetables. There are dairy farms too.

FARMS IN THE SOUTH

The soil is poor in the south. There is much less rain. They grow a special wheat for making pasta. They grow lemons and oranges and keep animals.

Some farmers in the south keep sheep in the hills. The south is dry, so grass for the sheep to eat only grows slowly.

Italy sells a lot of tinned foods, especially tinned tomatoes.

LIVING IN SICILY

THE CUNSOLO FAMILY

Salvatore and Anna Cunsolo live in Sicily, an island off the coast of southern Italy. They have two boys, Vincenzo (who is thirteen) and Nicola (who is two) and two girls, Luana (who is seventeen) and Zaira (who is nine).

The family live in a flat in the town of Catania. Salvatore's nephew, Enrico, lives with them too.

The family on their balcony. Look how narrow the street is.

In the mornings, Salvatore likes to have a cup of coffee in a café.

The family are eating pasta with cheese and vegetables.

THE FAMILY'S DAY

Salvatore grows oranges and olives on a small farm. The farm does not make much money so he paints and decorates houses to make more money. Anna works as a teacher and Enrico teaches too. He teaches ballet.

While the grown-ups work, the children go to local schools. They all eat together in the evening. Anna does the shopping at the local street markets.

Enrico helps to pick oranges at harvest time.

Some farmers sell their fruit and vegetables from the backs of their cars at the street market.

Children playing football at breaktime in Vincenzo's school.

17

ITALIAN SHOPS

DAILY SHOPPING

Most Italian shops are still small shops run by one family. They sell different sorts of food. Some sell bread, others sell fruit, meat, cakes or ice cream.

People also shop in open-air or covered markets. They can buy fresh food from local farms. They can also buy clothes and household **goods** in some markets.

A market stall in Sicily. Markets are a good place to buy fresh local food cheaply.

You can now use a computer to order Italian things directly from Florence!

CITY SHOPPING

Italian cities, like Rome, have big shops full of expensive clothes and jewellery. They also sell things that their area is famous for, things that **tourists** want to buy.

OPENING HOURS

Most shops open at 9 am and close at about 1 pm. They stay closed for the hottest part of the day. They open again at about 4 pm and stay open until 7 pm.

This street of shops is in Rome. The shops sell expensive clothes and jewellery.

ITALIAN FOOD

People all over the world eat Italian food. Pizza, pasta and ice cream are all Italian dishes.

Many people like to eat outside when the weather is good.

PASTA

Pasta is made from flour, salt and water. Spinach or tomato paste can be added to give it colour. Pasta can be made into lots of shapes – tubes, bows or even flat sheets. Spaghetti is long, thin pasta. You eat pasta with a sauce made from meat, vegetables or fish.

Mozzarella cheese is made from buffalo milk.
It melts when it is cooked.

LOCAL FOOD

Italians mostly eat food that is grown locally. Olive oil and tomatoes are used in all Italian cooking, because they are grown everywhere. Northern Italian recipes use meat because of the dairy farms there. Southern recipes use fish — there are more fishermen in the south.

People usually eat their pasta with parmesan cheese on top.

Italians often finish their meal with ice cream, which was invented in Italy over 200 years ago. They also drink coffee. Espresso coffee is very dark and strong. Cappuccino coffee is made with strong coffee and lots of frothy milk. It has chocolate sprinkled on the top.

Lunch is often salad with cold meat, cheese and bread.

21

MADE IN ITALY

Italy sells all sorts of **goods** to other countries, from food and drink to clothes and cars. Goods that are sold to other countries are called **exports**.

Venice is famous for the glass goods made there. The glass is melted and shaped by blowing down a tube.

FAMOUS GOODS

Italian cloth was famous hundreds of years ago. It still is. Italian clothes are famous too. People come from all over the world to look at the clothes made by Italian **designers**.

Italy also exports less expensive goods. You can buy Italian pasta, tomatoes, olives, anchovies and wine in shops all over the world.

FACTORIES

Most of the big factories that prepare food for export are in the north of Italy. So are the factories that make other famous Italian exports, like cars and motorbikes. Many people move north to work in these factories.

The car being made in this factory is a Ferrari. It is one of the most expensive cars in the world.

GETTING AROUND

Italy has never been easy to reach or to travel in, because of the mountains. You can now reach Italy from Europe on roads or railways that go over the Alps or tunnel through them.

ROADS

Italy has a motorway system which runs all the way to the far south. But, even now, smaller roads creep along the sides of mountains and are dangerous because they are narrow and need repairs.

Italian cities have lots of traffic. The quickest way to get around is often on scooters like these.

RAILWAYS

The big cities are joined by a fast train service. People in smaller places use slower, less frequent trains. Rome has an underground railway system.

BOATS AND PLANES

There are ferry services to the Italian islands and also to Greece. In the south, local people travel by boat.

Italy has international airports in its biggest cities. Business people and tourists often come to Italy this way.

You have to pay to use the motorways in Italy. The money pays for repairs.

The motorways around Rome and other big cities are very busy. Pollution is damaging the beautiful old buildings.

SPORTS AND HOLIDAYS

SPORTS

Italians like to watch and play football, tennis and basketball. There are bicycle races on most weekends. Lots of Italians enjoy skiing. Many children learn to ski when they are very young.

TIME OFF

Sport is not the only thing that Italians do for fun. They do less active things too. They watch TV, play cards, sit at outdoor cafés and talk. Many families go for a walk after their evening meal, stopping to talk to people along the way.

Venice is built in a lagoon (lake). It has canals instead of roads. People travel by boat. These gondolas (boats) are carrying tourists.

Tourists like to shop in Italian markets. There are lots of stalls in this market selling goods made from leather.

HOLIDAYS

People from all over the world go to Italy for their holidays. There are lots of things to do. The weather is good, too.

Some **tourists** want to visit museums and art galleries. They want to look at old buildings and remains from the time of the **Roman Empire**. They can visit cities like Rome or Florence.

Tourists who want a holiday by the sea can go to one of the many holiday resorts all along the coast of Italy. Others prefer to go into the mountains for the lovely views and skiing in winter.

Many tourists visit the town of Pisa to see the Leaning Tower. It was built in 1173, and has been leaning further and further over ever since!

FESTIVALS AND ARTS

At this Roman Catholic festival in the south of Italy, the priests are praying for rain. The farmers need the rain for their crops to grow.

FESTIVALS

Some festivals are held for religious reasons. Most Italians are Roman Catholic. Some are held all over Italy, like Easter. On New Year's Day, the Pope (the head of the Roman Catholic Church) gives a world-wide blessing.

Some religious festivals are smaller. Most towns have their own saint who has a special saint's day. On this day people say special prayers and carry a statue of their saint through the streets.

ARTS

Italian music and painting is famous all over the world. **Renaissance** artists and **sculptors** are still famous. Michelangelo (1475–1564) was a painter and sculptor. He painted the ceiling in the picture, while lying on his back. It took him four years.

This ceiling, in the Sistine Chapel in Rome, was painted by Michelangelo.

Italian opera music is famous, too. Many of the world's most famous opera singers come from Italy. Pavarotti is a famous opera singer today. He sings all over the world.

Leonardo de Vinci is another famous Renaissance artist. He painted the Mona Lisa.

ITALY FACTFILE

People

People from Italy are called Italians.

Capital city

The capital city is Rome.

Largest cities

Rome is the largest city. Nearly three million people live in Rome. Milan is the second largest city and the third largest city is Naples.

Head of country

The head of Italy is called a president.

Population

There are about 57 million people living in Italy.

Money

The money people use is called the lira.

Language

People speak Italian. The Italian alphabet does not have the letters j, k, w, x and y.

Education

Children have to go to school between the ages of six and fourteen.

GLOSSARY

active working

canals rivers that have been made by people

designers people who make up new styles of clothes

erupt when a volcano throws out ash and lava (melted rock from under the earth's surface)

exports things that are sold to other countries

extinct not around anymore

goods things that people have made

peninsula a piece of land with water almost all around it

polluted when the air, water or land has been made dirty

Renaissance a way of talking about the time 1300–1600, when art and learning was very important. Italy was important at this time.

Roman Empire the Romans were people who, starting from Rome in Italy, took over much of Europe and other parts of the world from about 750BC to AD300

sculptors people who make statues or other pieces of art

tourist someone who goes to a place for a holiday

volcano a mountain that sometimes erupts

INDEX